THE MAY
FIGURES

THE MAY FIGURES

CHRIS PREDDLE

THE **BLACK SPRING**
PRESS GROUP

First published in 2022
An Eyewear Publishing book, The Black Spring Press Group
Grantully Road, Maida Vale, London W9,
United Kingdom

Typeset with graphic design by Edwin Smet
Author photograph Jean Bashford
Cover photograph Chris Preddle
The cover photograph shows may trees in flower in Rake Lane in Holme, West Yorkshire.

ISBN 978-1-913606-08-4

BLACKSPRINGPRESSGROUP.COM

for
Jacqueline

CONTENTS

I

II

III

I

A HARE

A hare, look, loping alone in a field at Charity Farm,
lepus, leaper, lope-hare,
lagomorph, unhurried.
Hare, of your charity, inform me
of the Queen of Hares, heard of
in grassland ungrazed and unharrowed.

TETHYS

Tethys rose out of the sea for him
as he walked away silenced on the beach. I am the Tethys Ocean.
You are the all-at-a-loss, for whom

I broke up All-Earth or C-shaped Pangaea
and pushed away Gondwana from Laurasia. They broke apart with seacries
who had been joined.

You might, I suppose, be Chryses
the priest of Apollo, or the youth who sat on the rocks one summer,
or any Chris in a crisis.

I brought the continent Cimmeria
for you to sit here. I made this southern coast
for you to mourn in Europe. I too may seem

diminished, to this Mid-Earth Sea. Human, accost
the shingle god who aggrieves the sea-hem,
the one the waves accuse and break themselves against.

SAPPHO

What is it, Sappho,
you suffer now, my goddess asked, so far

into the future? I answered, Scholars keep asking and asking
about lacunae in my poem of Tithonus aging,

gaps or lagoons in the papyrus. Whatever belonged
in the vacancies, I've quite forgotten – I live so long

through the iniquity of time.
Quit me, time.

My arms are paperwhite on the bed. I am papery thin as
Tithonus.

But whenever you, my goddess Dawn,
like a wife come down to me, your rose-red clothes undone,

I am like you goddess immortal,
as those gappy papyrus poems of mine may tell.

HELOISE

To him especially hers, she writes who is singularly his.
You hid me pregnant in a habit of Christ
as we fled all France to the coast of Brittany, an Heloise
none should recognise, all-veiled, a bride of Christo.
At Argenteuil we raised my habit
in a corner of the nuns' refectory. There's nothing else
my body thinks of. I should be a modish demoiselle in a boat-hat
by the Seine, where Monet will set his easel.

But we in this early time,
each in her own cell or room, as far
as we see across the habited earth or known oecumene,
all serve like serfs the divine economy.
You cite me scriptures and prescripts in your letter. I am
mere soul to save. That's what my body was for.

SARAH

Sarah rodeo-rides (yippee) on her farm quadbike
instead of the Holme white horse. No longer a bareback kid

or the White Goddess or bare Godiva,
I'm an ATV diva.

A horse may become a chalky hill figure,
court-huntswomen will ride in Dior shades or fragrances by Hilfiger,

but I give you a quadbike for a sign.
Though utile as a ute, let it signify

the making of shapes
with its trailered load or its own track or a drive of sheep,

any artefacture or forming. The bale of haylage
that I bring by horsepower and haulage

is a sign of all I bring to bear
against those impositions I used to bear.

MARY

In three days (so Mary to Ken) you have read to us
at Derwentwater in the rain under canvas
all *Paradise Lost* –
makers we are, not losers of sweet converse.

Our tentative tendful conversation
makes up for the mythic certitudes we're rid of,
for God like his own angel fallen. In the new unconversion
how we miss our Persian paradises lost.

Make us instead no Eden but a Persian
sweetwater garden, four-square, walled and willowed,
whose quarters are the quadrants of the world.

We form its verdant order with a passion,
to make up for all outside that's adverse and arid.
Converse in this pavilion or tent, and read to us.

JACQUELINE READING

How your reading figure draws to mind
      a curve at your back, angles
at your midriff, hips and elbows, an equilateral triangle
      under your knees, the slope of your lap
and the ever-continuing line of the thinking mind.
Jacqueline reclining, how every tangent and loop of you
      is drawn to your book, a book on
illhumoured humans I'd turn the abstract curve of your back on.

Goodhumoured hens I sing, seven Rhode Island
      reds, triangular forms
that tip and tilt at grains on Charity Farm.
      No – not hens, not even Carola's
that caroller of hens, or Emily's seven highland
henriettas – I sing of a beautiful construct, Euler's
      equation, I sing like a swain
how e to the $i\,\pi$ is equal to minus one.

Let Euler's e be the base of the infinite exponential
      curve of your back; let i,
that unit we barely imagine, be you, though I
      barely imagine your complex plane;
let π and I be constant, though I'm not transcendental.
How your inclining figure, like Euclid, would explain
      we too may touch the abstract,
make in our humours an artefact, a sign of the absolutes that attract us.

UNDRESS

Undress, all seawhite,
at the sea's edge. The white sea
breaks on you, on edge.

II

TO AL ALVAREZ, NOVEMBER 2010

At the tale-end of the voyage-tale
we're back, as you say, to lovers we never left, to Donne
undone by God, and Yeats with spirits on the tiles,
and the Mael Duin of muledom, Muldoon.

A poem is a search for values
by way of connections: your own verse-toil and mine
as much as Sappho's songs and Sylvia's.
We all, as we hoke our graves, would hoke up meaning.

We all, in a single time and always, tell
our search-tale. I believe in the communion
of sonnets, Hill with Herbert, Wystan with Will.

Converse in verse with a shade you miss, as I with Peter Levi's
who's crossed the Hodder. We're never done,
as we search for signs, with the give and take of lovers.

TO KEN BELL, DECEMBER 2010

Isaak, angler, compleat
with fishing tackle and basket by a river, contemplates

a book, as he sits on a stump by the river of Anglican thought,
on your postcard from Winchester. He has unthought

whatever would unquiet his study, in that stained-glass window.
He may read his own

Lives of Donne and Herbert, Wotton and Hooker,
whom God had by the mouth with fish-hooks.

As we go the way of all fish,
you and I and Isaak, genteel or Joe, elfin or oafish,

I would unfeel the anxieties that fail me, unbe
whatever angular I've been,

but I do not contemplate for myself, even as I seek it
by Anglican angleworms, the quietness of Isaak.

TO KATRINA PORTEOUS, JANUARY 2011

I wrote from Holme in snow, Oh, I skulk
glum as a skull, numbskull-
and-bone in a catacomb of snow,
perished to the Muse in my snow barrow.

You wrote from Beadnell under snow, No, figure
how long it takes to be configured
to a new music, as you take hecatombs of snow-
white oxen to the Muse in her snow bower.

Impatient, yes! I've seen her likeness here,
the girl on a sled in Europe before the Great War,
I know her passion set down with a last dispassionate clearness.

Perish thou and I and oxherd
and all who saw her on the snowy hill (how great they were),
so long as each new music is heard.

TO GRAHAM RANSOM, FEBRUARY 2011

That number 89
is where Jacqui and I are x and y on each side
of the equation, where no one, no

divisor in a visor shall divide us;
that our prim number is a prime suspect
in a sequence only increasing like pairs of rabbits, into the void

from 89 to no finality; that however they're spooked
it's rabbits without end
whose neighbouring numbers, as your rabbits of Brookhouse expect,

closer and closer tend
to the Divine Proportion, the Golden Ratio;
all this, as we tire the Lune with talking, my mathematician friend,

all this, as we measure your lettuce bed for rabbit-proofed enclosure,
may imply that even I, unnumbered human,
closer tend and closer

to a steady state between black and sanguine humour;
that mood by mood, bad mood after bad
I am perfected (coneys, humour me)

to peace, peace; that we have borrowed
a little contentment, Graham, until that festival returns
(Adonis O is dead in a lettuce bed,

pummel your breasts, girls, make your tunics tattered and torn);
that number 89
is where I and she are a and b in a happy ratio, sine or tan.

TO ED REISS, JUNE 2012

Detached as you are, your sort, from trafficke,
come down from the leaky reservoir on Kiln Bent Road
where JN Bentley
constructs an overflow with a constant flow of trucks,

come down the bent or hill
to Netherley Clough and its fluent beck. On the bank we'll discuss
the discursive discourse, debouch and cursus and excursus
of late Geoffrey Hill.

Everything flows. I cry, Such havocke!
But Heraclitus in tears, you tell me, would never revoke
a molecule. As the becks go seaward

Hill at the top of his bent makes form
from formless. Now then, let us on a bentgrass bench or form
make an ever-this and ever-itself from confluent words.

TO ROBIN BONNER, NOVEMBER 2014

You live, I thought, in a socialist Little Gidding,
with little or no God in,

a commune or communion of England's
Left, the last left. Marx and Engels

already foresaw Lenin with a besom
sweep off the earth's bosom

kings, capitalists and clergy. Arms and the bank
they sang as they fell away, but still they climb back on.

You live, I thought, in an order of peace,
where the languages and anguish of Europe pass through.

This least of times and latest age
of our long radicalism, in its dotage

labours to an end. Like Nicholas Ferrar in fire and fairness,
you live the better world-idea already foreseen.

TO MARK ROBSON, DECEMBER 2014

Mark him, the eternal mariner
enters the underparts of Europe like an unmannerly

amoeba, Odysseus
in every port and aperture from Odessa

to the Baltic, Romany Aeneas,
Onassis berthed in his ownership in Nice.

The seas he navigates
seagird our conflicts, Europa bullish in a navy skirt.

Mark you, as you sail the seamarks
of Sounion, Tainaron with its pharos, and St Mark's

to the fair Hesperides – no, to Finisterre and the Gulf of Finland,
as you skirt the agonistic land

find us an edge or hem
of Europe, a hermit ledge, humans at peace on a seaholm.

III

THE MAY FIGURES

I

If you, I or Under-the-Sky came down
from Issues Road and Meal Hill
with human anxiety like a hem undone,

if we came to Holme
and Watery Lane and Rake Lane
and lifted the hood of selfhood like a helm,

how the external, matter earthen and carnal,
comes up against us. That city-state
of Holme and its habitations, cattle, fruit trees, cornland

and whatever else may be numerically stated,
are what is. Though we ourselves
name and number them under the sky, they are constituted

that which avails us,
they contain what also is. As we decline
down Meal Hill and Rake Lane, we meet there other selves,

Achilles in his helm, a sweet colleen
of the Clyde or Caryae or the County Down,
all the hooded and lost, and new Helen in Jacqueline.

And came Jacqueline inland to a seagreen porch
in Holme, riverlass of the Greenock shipyards
or holme, naiad
of the Clyde and Bert's café on the Esplanade.
As the tide came in, shallows and shoals disappeared
and she could gain no purchase.

And came inland to a mere pond,
though even a garden pond, a tadpole-
puddle may also serve
to reflect a view of the mighty reservoir
under Twizle Head moor. Came to a lilypad-pool
and opened
in the sun, nymph
of the swimming Nymphaeas.

II

Misshapen pines and firs
are thinned
on Meal Hill, as the Emperor Taizu thinned
his Chinese pines, his civil service.

The servant pine-needles
sing aloud, though wind-flagged trees are examined, failed
and in all their imperfections felled.
They need us less.

Misshapen firs and pines,
tree-nymphs to themselves, sing to the Emperor Song Taizu,
Great Ancestor. Not one repines

as we repine on Meal Hill. What we start from
is their sylvan separateness from us, that we've to use
to make for ourselves a shape or form.

III

Tell me now, Muses who live on Olympus,
of those who live below
the high transmitter of Holme, beside
Rake Lane at a rakish angle, above
Rake Dyke in its bed under the moors.
Their human hill of the Muses,
a cut above
that beck, descends in the end to its bedside,
lies low
in the valley where the water limps.

Turner, precisian and point-device,
construed a measured passage of Homer
each morning, as if heroic virtue and vice

would complement a punctilious Christian humour.
Each afternoon under monastic oaks
he mouthed the office. And to precisely him

the frogs in Monks Pond croaked Ko-ax, ko-ax!
Did Christ preserve Achilles? Or vice versa?
Uncelibate frogs, go drown your cog and coax.

Russell, wiser than the sophist owls
of Athens, a pedagogue and philologue
of Sappho's inflected forms and soft-lived vowels,

inflected like a verb his Catholic leg
to any resin Mary in a cloak of azure.
He'd innocence enough to have sung of Lalage,

unharmed among humans. O read your Frazer,
no Queen of May, no Corn-maid will avail us,
not the great Mother Goddess of Western Asia.

And came upriver from her northern coast
against the swim
of things, against the shallows and shoals that would assume
they were grounds for something. Swam like a Jacqueline Cousteau
in the schools
of fish and scholars, sophies
and Sufis and cod philosophers.
Emerged upriver at Holme in her mermaid scales
and her own sophrosyne,
her passionate mindfulness. Someone had there foreseen her.

Kate, dramaturge of the Demiurge,
uncasual casuist, divine
of case-divinity at the marge
with morals, make us a play, a sign

to avail one failing. On a hoop of grass
I cannot do what Katy did,
sick and saintly. No-hoper of grace,
grasper at culms, tettigoniid,

I'd imitate your own good muse's
cause and conscience. Articulate
our pity and fear. Mime eases us.
Make us a form cathartic, Kate.

Graham by math and footrule rakes
his courtyard garden of Japan.
He measures the world, Pythagoras
in ten square feet. Ah, Graham-san,

the golden ratio has determined
form. Elliptic stones are held
in gravel loops. A shapen pine
leafs and unleafs, its shape compelled

like clouds. A granite snow-lantern shines
no light. Snow light. Russell would say,
from form or an abstract proposition
something's taken away.

And came to a Pennine upland
unlit in the clouds. Cloud
occluded
the sheep, grass and ploughland
and Holme's high transmitter of knowledge
whose monitory red
mast lights could not be read
for the low cloud. Acknowledged
in the cloud of unknowing, do that in thee is,
and she would,
for all the devils go crazy, alle feendes ben wood
when you do this.

IV

The Three Graces came, David Jones's
       muses, pencil-drawn
like souls in gouache and pastel. What David has joined
three in one portrait, would separate, indrawn
to each her inturnèdness. They came from the unParnassus
       of Harrow undancing, to where
       Jacqueline had come, her own sea-person,
sea grace by seagrass shaded. Sing them there,
four, with paeans. Not inward graces, these
are signs, he said, human and made, of the other that is.

Tell me now, muses who live in Holme,
       how an inturned artefact, an arty
fiction of a poem, or Petra sullen and solemn
in a picture, has virtu and power, Parnassian areté,
outdoes the body upright. Petra happy
       at Capel-y-ffin would weave,
       fine-weave her cloth, her body a hoop,
all curves he might unclothe, or hoped to wive.
She went to the muslin shades. Petra morose
is made over to us, more real than our goodmorrows.

And Prudence he loved, carver and curver of stone
       in a man's workshop, apprentice
Artemis, arty miss of the Chilterns, unvirgin
huntress. Though man is 'the darling of Prudentia', Prudence
would not take him for hers, wholly marry-me-not
       at Pigotts between the wars.
       O prudent Providence divine – may not
this underling of Art have peace? What other she was,
green girl of the beechwood, killer of deer,
what other, he asked, since more than herself, like Christ my dear.

And Valerie last he loved. Gwener fair
        looked back to the Roman sea
she rose like foam from. Whitethorn Guinevere
rode out, a May figure. In a new romance
a girl with downcast eyes came to his pension
        in Harrow, a girl in a scoop-
        neck dress more purple than peonies Parnassian.
He made her portrait – that dress her cassock or cope,
a hoop dispassionate. By other realities caressed,
he suffered in his own. Whom Venus touched, Christ crossed.

Came Jacqueline inland. Jacq-in-the-Green
        came riding, Queen of May now,
hawthorn white and green, in flower and grain
more than she is. Throw Death in a river or mere now.
New patterns of things formed behind her
        as she rode, the poet's conceits
        made person. Attendant truths did hand her.
Came down Meal Hill, past Abigail's, to the setts,
to Glenys and Brian's. Glenys had thinned to a shade.
Came muse and grace, kept her self, shared more than she had.

V

And came to a hinterland, a mind-and-heartland
of moors, which loomed like headlands
of the Clyde hardly moored
to their coast. She might have once herself unmoored
coastwise; Celtic, she was of sea people
whom the sea impels
to its edge. Came landways to Holme
where the moors lay in column
like the Clyde's warships made lame
in their sea-holme.

And came to a snowland, the white of an eye
of Arthur felled
in his imperfections, his length all England. On a snowfield
Ever-Since or you or I
went about in anxiety. Our history
has failed;
we decline, we noble knyghtes tinfoiled,
to doo after the good and leve the evyl; our island-story
has no moral. Came
among the helmed uneasy Is on an icefield
fouled
like the field of Camlann. Came
hawthorn, white. Came as the other, she or Who-May-Be
who is whatever value there may be.

And came to a windland where the helm-
wind of Holme
wound her in a windingsheet. As if at a making of hay
they had been made hay of,
bales

on a field of bale-
stour. The bale wrapper like a woman lifted
and wound them in black film.
They were black cattle with cut-off limbs,
cut back and left.

And came to a rainland. Galled by the rain
a Roman, or Graham
measured ground for a camp by math and groma,
surveyor's rod. Too far, this, from the Gaulish Rhine.
And Rod on a Caterpillar in the Pennine rain
dug up Charity Farm by diagram,
made heaps or grumi
in a line, and sank a field drain.
Celt of the Clyde, she saw how more had come
than earthen forms from a maker
of earthen forms. He makes
an ideal, for us who come
to be laid like waterpipes in this terrain.
He makes the eternal Mediterranean.

VI

I am not for England. I have no idea
what England or being English might be for.
Let Issues Road come down from Ida.
Young Katy, risen like a noble fir,
trots with her sheep in Holme, uno pastourèlo
grieving, or Goethe's Schäferin Scapine
sheep's-eyed. The 'ego' is in pastoral.
Herd us, Katy, under the cosmic pine.

VII

I am the East-West vagrant, viandante,
Jew and musician, with a shouldered viol;
midway and more, ebreo e musicante,

I make a music (gigue) that will avail.
We shall be painted on an umber ground
for a ground bass, a brown on which we travail

all Europe. The pink sky is a dancing ground
(chaconne) of suns and halfmoons. An onion dome
turns in the distance, Christ-go-Mary-go-round

(maestoso) on a red plain. To play for a dime
makes shape and order. Merely to walk (andante)
is belief that peace shall come, at random.

I am the Miriam itinerante,
Miriam-go-round. I bend into the wind
as the bass viol or cello concertante

bends to the player. I hold a baby, wound
in mummy white, curved as the halfmoons curve
over my shoulder. Midway, you never warned me,

Jew musician, how each place ever recurs,
old Troy, the roads Alexander rode,
where Charlemagne sleeps. I have seen the oxbow curves

of the Somme like hoops go round. I wear rosered
for the rosy halfmoon. Ebraica e migrante,
I am the curve of kindness on our road.

I am the baby, halfmoon shape,
half moon, poised on a hip, on a hope
of peace. Bebè, bambina-go-round,
I am carried as an ayre above the ground
over the heaps of history. I am Astyanax
thrown from a wall of Troy. On Kristallnacht
I broke like a shopfront. In Sarajevo
I starved in a cellar. Sorrow-I-Have,
go round, go round like a hoop or a hope.
So said the baby, halfmoon shape.

VIII

And came south, from the saltwater Battery Baths
of Greenock, to a green wood sun-
leafed in Aix. Cézanne
would paint her forever among the river bathers.

And came a colleen of Caryae, caryatid
who upheld the porch
of the sky.
Sky
pressed on her aortic arch,
oppressed the columns of her carotid,
such pressure all through
from the very fillet and embroidered band
of Sardis in her hair
to a slender
sandal,
such a burden should have overborne her,
bent her with a Grecian bend.
For what you suffer heart's-longing eats her through.

And came like Thetis inshore, broke open
the sea-roof, breached the suff and surface
of the sea-tiles. Did it not suffice
her sea-children died young, like sea-wrack broken up?

And came ashore at Cyprus. In the Dome Hotel
in a queensize bed or sea-bed
she listened to the sowff
and suffer
of the sea. To love and be loved is not so bad.
In the green McCartney dress I'm tall
as a cypress. Stood at the pier-glass and pinned
her yellow hair, with the sea-windows open.

And came uphill to the Abbey of Peace
in ruins, its medieval stone
stolen
like peace of mind. She was taken piece by piece.

And came south, as one in a myth
came to an island of serviceable pines
whose pins and needles
slid and sledded her down to a beach. No needless
goats or Pan
went down to her naked rock. The bay opened its mouth
to the quop and slop
of the sea at the foot of the great sea-slope.
And fifty nereids came ashore
and sang her a sea-name like their own.
By that and this she shall be known,
nereid sunning by the green sea-door.

IX

27000 BCE

Let the first figure be a figurine.
Ice Age woman of Moravia hipped
with hoops of flesh, O rhombus-in-the-round
of flesh, fleshhood of the human process,
a maker on a meadow-holme made you
blank as a helm of face. O Stone Age fair,
bicone of flesh, you were no sign unless
a person, some particular Venus
loved by a maker in Moravia.

2800 BCE

Gilgamesh King of Uruk made these walls
as if to keep out Death. Look at the brickwork
kiln-fired, walk along the parapet.
He felled the Cedar Forest, killed like disease
cedar cadavers, killed the cedar-hoarder
Humbaba fatter than a banker by
the fat Euphrates. He killed Ishtar's Bull.
He killed my crew of Stone Ones. He made me sail
the Ocean to its edge, to find distant
Utnapishtim, the everliving human.

Utnapishtim thus, courtoyse and humayne,
on's couch. The gods have to themselves detain'd
life; death conferr'd mankinde, and seal
the time of it. Gilgamesh, retourne to Babel
(and take this whoreson ferryman Urshanabi
should never have brought you). Any mayfly had

our time under the sun. I am ill at ease
in Dilmun, untimely human here. Depart,
who can. Content you in your temporal work.
Gilgamesh King of Uruk made those walls.

1200 BCE

Nereids came ashore like Scarborough gulls
promenading. Thetis on the harrowed sand
foresaw, to seaward of the blithe sea-girls,
Achilles and the anvil ships at hand.

1190 BCE

Not such a no-use burden on the earth –
rather, the earth
bears you on her body-curve. Upheld,
with all your grief exhaled,
be mindful
how every organ, even the full mind,
is safekept in the bone-cove or safehold
of the body. You have with every breath, inhaled
force
for the outcome you wish to enforce.

Yet the earth in her passage will heel over
and turn on her heel
even from you. Whatever closes
the doors of sense and art and love, discloses
the door to the afterlife.
After life
you will meet the singers of Troy, from the first
who sang your anger, to Michael the shanachy of Belfast

on the machair of the blest inheld
like sea-marram heeled in.

600 BCE

Aphrodite Nevertodie,
Aphrodite Withedeceit
loves you, Sappho. You shall see
her face immortal, hers of Cyprus in the sea.
As in the upper world you've sung
lovers, liars, lemans, liers-by,
Aphrodite Artifice,
Aphrodite Forceofheart –
so in the underworld for your deserving
Serve me, Sappho songs and tortoise lyre,
you shall be honoured, no less
than Aphrodite, by the flown and honourless.

200 CE

Let the next figure be in low relief
sculpted. Eudemos the seatrader's tomb
in Lycian Olympos, in our grief
his fellow citizens erected. Whom
the seas unself and separate from us,
whom the Euxine afflicted, is beyond
the wind's assistance and the daylight's. Form us,
seanymph, to the term we spend in bond.

590

Shirin of Armenia on her road in Persia
paused. A minor river, no Oxus,
passed her like time with a passing passion.
Herself the other, time's excess, a nexus,
she bathed, and on a bank lay, nixie uncovered,
kufic. The flowering Persian desert
upheld her, a divan to her. A willow curved over
and discovered her. Leaves (we leaf for you) desired her.
Khosrow of Persia on an ivory horse
paused, and desired her. As I pass through time
I betray each cause and principle, rehearse
every expedient. Let her be the term
I keep to. I am King of Kings. Shirin
untimes us. We are held always in this scene.

1150

The servant pines are at their song.
The larkspur look like her as she walks along,
silent, in blue. They bend
with the wind and break; those she cannot mend
drop in her hall. Today she cannot choose
a hairpin, even less a form or shape to use.

The serviceable pines go down
to a lake, as if to swim away. Her gown
swishes in the anxious
needles. Even such beauty as Xi Shi's
went down to a lake of gauze. She will care
for the larkspur, and lifts a hand to shape her hair.

1293

Girl
crimson in cramoisy, prefigure
that Love Unfailing, which could yet forgo
a knight who follows and fails, as Lancelot the grail.
She goes through banks of crimson balsam
naked under cramesy. For all my bella figura
the devil Belphegor
numbers me in his prime. Beat me for a Balaam's ass.
Madonna of the crimson moon I serve
for a saviour, though stars and planets dance like figures of May
for Him Whoever-He-Is.
Girl-Christ,
when sun and mindfulness have left me, let me not misfigure
how I, gathered like may, shall be caressed.

1415

Girl
cramoysin on the harbour-bar, be to us
Tianfei, sea-goddess of the treasure fleet.
Seamark, seaguide us to Malacca, Kollam,
Ormuz, Malindi, to the sea's uttermost
mark and margin. Twenty kings compelled
complied. We brought the west into the order
All Under Heaven, as a mariner
brought cramoisi to the seagirl Lin Moniang.

1432

Let the next figure, Leóndios Makhairás,
mourn for Cyprus. Panayía, let our Maker hear us
among the Greekless Moslems. We
were His East-West dominium in the sea,
sweet land
of Cyprus, between the woodlouse Thomists and
the sandflea monks of Syria. What a Christ-crusader king
we had once, havocking
the infidels of Asia! We have ruled
Jerusalem. Now I the servant of the king grow old,
and even the City,
goldleaf Byzantium may fall. Christós Sotír,
it is not in me to complete
my mythistoria of Cyprus. Contemplate
the course of things: no honest value lasts,
though all I've seen and heard should not with my time be lost.
I see both ways in time: our own King Janus
captive in Egypt, as the coining Genoese
exact us. Panayía of the Pines, I shall be wood, would lose
the expectation of Goodness here. We pines need less.

1647

Cape Cod
beckoned us over, crook'd like the forefinger of God.
We were His Separated. This month, seventeen
of our number die, the Governor wrote, yet we have not Satan
as do the popish. Lift up Bathsheba's kirtle,
be whipped at the cart's tail. We were near curtailed
quite, when the Indian corn we hoped to weather

withered
like faith gone hard. God
fed them out of the sea, he wrote, who saw His good
in our forbearance. We were not saved
not to profit and prosper. Even we His Saints
may raise the price of our corn and cattle
by a Puritan percent. Abandon your little curtilage
church-like in Plymouth. Where
grainland is like God extended, we are there.

1790

I, Sarah, of a sort Susanne, un jour
I married the old man, who saw me bathe
naked as a Mason jar.
He had standing in the salons of Bath
bas-bleu. Like any lightish Barbauld
I'd have written odes. I'd be a painted muse
of letters. O my Lady Bab.
I thought morality a Field of Mars,
piety militant. I live sad and long
without her. Only a person can endear
the times to us. This age of England
is coming to an end. I keep indoors.

1880

Herr Russell in retirement declined
seawards like a star figure
to the Baltic Sea, to the sands at Warnemünde
in the Kaiserreich, to a hooded beach-chair, testudo of wicker
inclined
at an angle of reflection to the anima mundi.

He thought of Hamburg and the demimonde
in his youth. She raised her two narcissus eyes.
Not God or goodness makes the great demand
upon you. No, it is I, is I, is I.
But he knelt to Art and Agape. Madonna
im Rosenhag received his sins and sighs.

Herr Russell in Warnemünde, under the wicker helm
of faith,
waited. White sails, narcissus-
ships tended towards Hamburg. Farther off,
shapes of the intellect, he thought, tend to an end or sea-holme.
He heard the waiting sea's sea-silences.

1900-

Somme the River God, angry in his hoops,
rose and ran over, in under the heaps
of the dead. O Meuse and Simoïs, Oise and Shatt al-Arab,
be a burial-sheet
for humans humans discarded; Amu River,
discover her, cover her.
Each figures more than herself – an afterlife
to be certain of. Whom sun and mind have left,
no makers making,
kiss, clip and clear them away, Congo, Mississippi and Mekong.

X

And had come Jacqueline to Rake Lane
for bluebells, in a pinafore
made plain for wartime, Persephone
descending. How many there were, in a rickrack line
on a hem of the wood. O Jacqueline,
humour us
with a slender ankle, they called who lived in humus.
Had come where came every Jack of the line.

And had come Jacqueline to Rake Lane
for violets. Viola Proserpina,
come down to us as we repine
for all that's other. We ache who've lain
in leafmould. Colleen
come inland, such anxious humours
in the leafbed inhume us.
Viola, avail us. More than you are, to us incline.

And had come Jacqueline to Rake Lane
for cowslips. We do not sleep. We duck our calix-
heads in saps and dugouts, not the likes
of those who lean
Elysian on their elbow. Tuber and root and corm
we are. Who led us here, mislaid us.
Cowslip lady ours,
let us become what you to us became.

And had come Jacqueline to Rake Lane
for maythorn; its branchy whiteflowered arms and legs
relaxed
in the wind, as a dead Christ might recline
on a marble lap. Had come
where Rake Lane went raking down to a wood. My lady, May lady,
we are all made
may figures here, and whiten the underwood to which we have come.

XI

As if in Rake Lane
we had maythorn enough, enough figures of may
for those gone down in a choric line
to Rake Dyke (where she came, may of May),
for those compelled pellmell in a black column,
an Acheron running, all who came
camp to camp, to bareness, to certainties at Auschwitz.
They settle in May on the maythorns ashwhite.

These are the may figures,
ash-made-other, whom the trees have beckoned back
so these, even these, may figure
the only axioms there are, the absolutes of Birkenau.
The kindness of absolutes is order. Presuming purpose,
makers of signs and forms, we suppose
whatever is surer than we are. The trees exist
on a lane, the lane on the earth, the earth on its axis tree.

Rake Dyke in a line-
dance dancefigure runs, runs on to the river Sola
bearer of ashes, burial urn in-
pours itself like a watergod into the Vistula
pours itself into the Baltic. The self is relative,
pours itself in a process. Its values
are abstract. Even the river (whose sweet colleen
came inland) dissolves to none, nowhere, at the sealine.

Beside the Baltic Sea
before the Achaeans came, a girl might pose
in a seaside frock. The boy she takes to,
talks about freedom. They sit on a rock, at peace.
Beside the Baltic Sea begin a beguine,
the dance to death of those on the seabank

compelled into the water. No-persons of the camps unfigured
any expectation of good, unnothings, none-figures.

      Unbodies of white ash
compel in-body us. To all she always comes
      as the may comes. It is her wish.
We are makers of forms and signs, for the real claims us,
those figures white-in-wood or death-in-may,
      and herself-of-may, may-other, may-
Persephone. Come down undone in a blackfigure line,
a hem of her frock, as if in Rake Lane.

ACKNOWLEDGEMENTS

Most of these poems, sometimes in earlier versions, appeared in the magazines *Irish Pages*, *Little Star*, *New Walk*, *Pennine Platform*, *Scintilla*, *Smartish Pace*, *Stand* and *The Yellow Nib*, or on the websites of the Manchester Poetry Prize and the Strokestown Festival.

I am most grateful to Clive Watkins for helpful suggestions, good discussions and wise advice.

Chris Preddle has retired from library work, in public libraries and with two childcare charities. He lived for many years in the village of Holme in West Yorkshire, on a windy shoulder of the Pennines. His second collection was *Cattle Console Him* (2010). He won the first PN Review Prize in 2017, has been shortlisted for the Manchester Poetry Prize (2012), was second in the Strokestown competition (2012), and won the Scintilla competition for shorter poems (2007). His work has appeared in many magazines in Britain and Ireland. He is translating the songs and poems of Sappho.